D1090356

Lea Michele

BY JODY JENSEN SHAFFER

The Child's World®

Published by The Child's World®
1980 Lookout Drive • Mankato, MN 56003-1705
800-599-READ • www.childsworld.com

Acknowledgments
The Child's World®: Mary Berendes, Publishing Director
The Design Lab: Cover and interior design
Amnet: Cover and interior production
Red Line Editorial: Editorial direction

Photo credits
Featureflash/Shutterstock Images, cover, 1, 25, 29; Chris
Pizzello/AP Images, 5; Seth Poppel/Yearbook Library, 7, 8; Bruce
Glikas/FilmMagic/Getty Images, 10; Joan Marcus/Photofest, 12;
Ilja Mašík/Shutterstock Images, 14; Richard Drew/AP Images,
16; Tina Fineberg/AP Images, 19; Helga Esteb/Shutterstock
Images, 21; David Drapkin/AP Images, 23; Randy Miramontez/
Shutterstock Images, 27

Design elements
Sergey Shvedov/iStockphoto

ISBN 9781614732945
LCCN 2012933735

Printed in the United States of America
Mankato, MN
July 2012
PA02128

Table of Contents

CHAPTER 1   Little Girl, Big Stage, 4

CHAPTER 2   Early Life, 6

CHAPTER 3   *Les Misérables*, 9

CHAPTER 4   *Ragtime*, 11

CHAPTER 5   High School and Summer Camp, 13

CHAPTER 6   *Spring Awakening*, 17

CHAPTER 7   *Glee*, 20

CHAPTER 8   More Success, 24

CHAPTER 9   The Future, 28

GLOSSARY, 30

FURTHER INFORMATION, 31

INDEX, 32

ABOUT THE AUTHOR, 32

Little Girl, Big Stage

A little girl dressed in rags walks alone onto a darkened stage. The stage looks like an inn. It has tables and chairs. The little girl is named Cosette. She has long, dark hair and dark, round eyes. Cosette carries a broom to the center of the stage. She looks tired. She does not smile. Her job is to sweep the floor. She does not want to sweep, but she has no choice. Cosette pulls the broom toward her, over and over again.

Softly, music begins to play. Cosette stops sweeping and looks toward the sky. Then she opens her mouth and sings.

There is a castle on a cloud,
I like to go there in my sleep,

Lea Michele's rise to fame began when she was just eight years old.

Aren't any floors for me to sweep,
Not in my castle on a cloud.

The girl on that stage was eight-year-old Lea Michele. She played Cosette in the musical *Les Misérables*. It was Lea's first time acting in a **Broadway** play. And her rise to stardom was only just beginning.

CHAPTER 2

Early Life

Lea Michele Sarfati was born on August 29, 1986, in the Bronx. That is part of New York. Lea's mother, Edith, was a nurse. Her father, Marc, owned a deli. Lea grew up as an only child in Tenafly, New Jersey. She attended elementary school at Rockland Country Day School. It was in Rockland County, New York.

Lea grew up near New York City. That city is known for its great plays and musicals. The most famous theaters are on a street called Broadway. Lea went to many shows in

Lea said she was fortunate she did not have any brothers or sisters. Otherwise, her parents might not have been able to support her career as much as they did.

Lea as a baby

Broadway theaters. She and a friend saw *Camelot,*
Cats, and *Phantom of the Opera*. Lea fell in love with the
theater. But she never thought she would become an

Lea did not think she would be an actress when she was growing up.

actress. She thought she would work as a waiter or a cashier in a grocery store. "I had that fake grocery store with the toy food and money," she said.

CHAPTER 3

Les Misérables

Lea began trying out for musicals in 1995. She did not mean to, though. One of Lea's friends went to an **open casting call**. Eight-year-old Lea tagged along. The **audition** was for the musical *Les Misérables*. The directors were looking for someone to play young Cosette. Lea was an outgoing kid. She thought it might be fun to play the part. So she ended up trying out. And she got the part!

Children teased Lea because of her last name. The end sounded like "fatty." She stopped using it when she began acting. Somebody asked for Lea's name at her first audition. She replied, "Lea Michele." "And I've been Lea Michele ever since," she said.

Lea got her acting start in the Broadway musical *Les Misérables.*

Lea liked to sing. But she did not know she could sing well until then. Lea's mom was surprised when she got the part. After all, Lea had never taken acting or singing lessons. Now she was playing young Cosette on Broadway.

CHAPTER 4

Ragtime

Lea liked performing in *Les Misérables*. So she decided to try out for more parts. Soon she went to an audition for the musical *Ragtime*. It was opening in Canada. Lea tried out for the part of a child character who had traveled to the United States with her father. Lea got the role. Within a month, Lea and her mother had moved to Toronto, Canada.

Lea acted in *Ragtime* for one year. Marin Mazzie played Lea's mother in the musical. Mazzie later said Lea was very determined and driven. Lea was very busy onstage in Toronto. She did not even have time to attend

In 2000, when Lea was 14, she acted in her first television show. She made a guest appearance on the drama *Third Watch*.

Lea in *Ragtime* on Broadway

school. Instead, Lea was homeschooled while there.

Lea and Edith returned to New Jersey after one year. Lea played the same character for another year. However, this time it was on Broadway. Lea finished acting in *Ragtime* in 2000.

CHAPTER 5

High School and Summer Camp

Lea went to Tenafly High School in New Jersey from 2000 to 2004. She took drama classes there. She also sang in an advanced choir. Lea starred in the school's production of *Carnival*.

Lea was often busy studying or acting on Broadway. She also worked in a bat mitzvah dress shop. Bat mitzvah is a rite of passage for Jewish girls. She cleaned and vacuumed there.

Lea had begun a successful acting career. However, she often had a hard time in high school. Some of Lea's classmates were wealthier

A glass display case at Tenafly High School is dedicated to Lea's success.

Lea acted in several Broadway plays in New York City.

than Lea's family. She sometimes struggled to fit in. Lea looked forward to her summers. That is when she attended Stagedoor Manor. It is a performing arts camp for kids between ten and 18 years old. Lea attended the camp each summer from 2000 to 2003.

Lea was already working as an actress. However, she was uncomfortable with her singing. She worked hard at the camp to get better. The camp needed somebody to sing the song "Tomorrow" during Lea's second summer. That is a famous song from the musical *Annie*. Lea volunteered. She was surprised at how well she did. For the first time, she could really belt out the songs. The sound was coming from deep inside her. "That was my turning point," Lea said.

Lea sings at an awards show.

CHAPTER 6

Spring Awakening

In 2000, Lea went to an open casting call for *Spring Awakening*. It was a musical featuring rock music. Lea got the **lead role** of Wendla Bergmann. She played Wendla on and off during her first three years of high school. *Spring Awakening* began in workshops and smaller theaters. Workshops help the **producers** address any problems before the play goes to a big theater.

Lea continued singing and acting. She played two characters

Lea met actor Jonathan Groff while doing *Spring Awakening*. They became best friends. Lea later helped Jonathan get a role on *Glee*.

in the musical *Fiddler on the Roof* before her senior year of high school. Lea also played the lead role in the *Diary of Anne Frank*. That play was at a regional theater in Maryland.

Lea had to make a decision about life after high school. She was accepted at the Tisch School of the Arts at New York University. However, she also had options to continue working as an actress. She decided to continue working. Lea graduated from high school and got an apartment in New York City.

In 2006, *Spring Awakening* moved to Broadway. Lea also had an opportunity to return to *Les Misérables* in 2006. The musical was re-opening on Broadway. Lea was offered the role of Eponine. However, she decided to stay with *Spring Awakening* instead. People recognized Lea for her good work in that musical. Television producer Ryan Murphy was one of them. He asked her to audition for *Glee*. It was a new musical comedy television show he was developing.

Lea poses with her *Spring Awakening* cast
mates in 2006.

CHAPTER 7

Glee

Lea had lived on the East Coast all of her life. In 2008, she left *Spring Awakening* and New York. The 22-year-old moved to Los Angeles, California. She wanted to be closer to Hollywood. She really hoped she could get a part on the television show *Grey's Anatomy*.

Lea had a hard time adjusting to Los Angeles. She did not feel she could be herself. She did not go to clubs like some of her friends. She liked quiet nights at home.

Lea first tried out for *Glee* in the fall of 2008. She had a terrible first audition. The pianist messed up her song and Lea got rattled. The producers laughed. Lea scolded

Lea dated Broadway actor Theo Stockman for more than a year beginning in 2009.

Lea arrives at a party celebrating season two of *Glee* in 2010.

them for it. She got even more laughs. They called Lea back for another look.

Lea nearly missed her next audition for *Glee*. Her car was hit while driving to the studio. She did not want to be late, though. So Lea left her wrecked car and ran. The decision paid off. She won the role of Rachel Berry. Rachel was the glee club captain.

Murphy created *Glee*. He said the part of Rachel Berry was written for someone like Lea. "Her talent was once in a lifetime," he said of Lea.

Lea sang "America the Beautiful" before the Super Bowl on February 6, 2011.

Lea agrees that she was perfect for the part. In fact, Rachel reminded Lea of herself growing up. Both were very driven and comfortable being themselves. "It was important to do what I believed in," Lea said.

Lea sings before the Super Bowl in 2011.

CHAPTER 8

More Success

Glee first aired in May 2009. It was an immediate hit with audiences and **critics**. Lea was a success, too. She was **nominated** for many awards. Among them was the Breakout Female Star award at the 2009 Teen Choice Awards. Lea was up for Best Performance by an Actress in a Television Series, Musical or Comedy at the 2010 Golden Globe Awards. And she was nominated for an Emmy

Lea filmed her first movie between the second and third seasons of *Glee*. It was called *New Year's Eve*. Many well-known actors were also in the movie. It came out on December 9, 2011. Most critics disliked the movie. However, it reached number one at the box office.

Lea arrives at the 2011 Emmy Awards.

in 2010. Lea also won the first-ever Triple Threat Award at Billboard's Women in Music event. She can sing, dance, and act.

Lea and the *Glee* cast released several albums of their music from the show. Many of the albums have reached platinum or gold status. A platinum album has sold more than one million copies. Gold means it sold more than 500,000 copies.

The *Glee* cast also performed at sold-out concerts. They toured in the United States, Canada, and Europe in 2010 and 2011. The Screen Actors Guild even nominated the cast for an award as the best cast in a comedy series in 2010, 2011, and 2012.

Lea always knew her time on *Glee* would not last forever. *Glee*'s creators intended that the characters would graduate. Rachel Berry was a senior in the spring of 2012. Lea said she was sad Rachel has to graduate. But Lea joked she could always come back as a substitute teacher!

Lea performs with the *Glee* cast in a concert.

CHAPTER 9

The Future

Lea is a talented actress, dancer, and singer. In 2012, she also began doing **voice-overs**. Lea played the voice of Dorothy in the animated *Dorothy of Oz*.

Lea accomplished a lot while she was still very young. She values all of the opportunities she has had to do different things. In the future, she plans to keep taking advantage of those opportunities. "I don't stop," Lea said. "I plan on playing every role on Broadway. I want to do movies, make music. *Glee* is only the beginning."

Lea is looking forward to playing many new and exciting roles in the future.

29

GLOSSARY

audition (aw-DISH-uhn): An audition is when actors try out for a role in plays or films. Lea went to an audition for *Les Misérables*.

Broadway (BRAWD-wey): Broadway is an area in New York City with 40 professional theaters seating 500 or more. Lea has acted in Broadway theaters.

critics (KRIT-iks): Critics are people who give opinions about a performance or a movie. Many critics immediately liked *Glee*.

lead role (leed rohl): The actor who plays the main character has the lead role in a production. Lea has played the lead role in productions.

nominated (NAH-muh-nate-id): To be named a finalist for an award is to be nominated. Lea has been nominated for many awards.

open casting call (OH-puhn kast-ing kawl): An open casting call is when all actors are invited to try out for a part. Lea went to an open casting call for *Les Misérables*.

producers (pruh-DOOS-urs): Producers find the money to make a film or play and supervise its production. The *Glee* producers laughed at Lea during her audition.

voice-overs (vois OH-vurs): Voice-overs are when an actor plays an animated character by performing the character's voice offscreen. Lea began doing voice-overs in 2012.

FURTHER INFORMATION

BOOKS

Balser, Erin, and Suzanne Gardner. *Don't Stop Believin': The Unofficial Guide to Glee.* Toronto, ON: ECW Press.

Rickman, Amy. *Gleeful!: A Totally Unofficial Guide to the Hit TV Series Glee.* New York: Villard.

WEB SITES

Visit our Web site for links about Lea Michele: childsworld.com/links

Note to Parents, Teachers, and Librarians: We routinely verify our Web links to make sure they are safe and active sites. So encourage your readers to check them out!

INDEX

awards, 24, 26

Glee, 17, 18, 20–22, 24, 26, 28

Les Misérables, 4–5, 9–10, 11, 18

Los Angeles, California, 20

Murphy, Ryan, 18, 22

New York, 6, 18, 20

parents, 6, 10, 11, 12, 14

Ragtime, 11–12

school, 6, 12, 13, 17–18

Spring Awakening, 17–18, 20

Stagedoor Manor, 14–15

ABOUT THE AUTHOR

Jody Jensen Shaffer is a poet and the author of several books for children. She writes from the home she shares with her husband, two kids, and dog in Missouri.